A
Faithful Heart

Daily Guide for Joyful Living

SALLY DYCK

Leader Guide by Sally D. Sharpe

ABINGDON PRESS
Nashville

A FAITHFUL HEART: DAILY GUIDE FOR JOYFUL LIVING LEADER GUIDE

ISBN 978-1-426-71083-4

10 11 12 13 14 15 16 17 18 19—10 9 8 7 6 5 4 3 2 1
MANUFACTURED IN THE UNITED STATES OF AMERICA

Contents

Introduction:

How to Lead *A Faithful Heart*

A Faithful Heart: Daily Guide for Joyful Living is a resource designed to help you and other women who gather with you to cultivate a faithful heart—a heart that is continually growing in faithfulness to God, in love, and in joy. As you make your way through the readings and gather together weekly for discussion and sharing, you will identify and explore eight characteristics of a faithful heart and recognize how to strengthen these in your daily living. You will discover that a faithful heart is, and is always striving to be,

> *Passionate*
> *Called*
> *Holy*
> *Equipped*
> *Joyful*
> *Loving*
> *Learning*
> *Authentic*

Throughout this eight-week journey, Mary, the mother of Jesus, serves as a biblical example of a faithful heart. Too often Mary gets lost in the nativity scene and is shrouded with all kinds of doctrinal questions. Yet Mary demonstrated her growing, faithful heart as she trusted God in bearing Christ into the world, learned from him throughout his earthly ministry, and was counted among his followers in the early church. For this reason, each week's readings begin by focusing on Mary and how she exemplified one of these eight characteristics of a faithful heart.

Of course, there are many women, like Mary, who demonstrate a faithful heart—women from history and literature as well as contemporary women, including the women in your own group. As you gather together for study and discussion, you will have the opportunity to recall and recite the faithfulness of other women, as well as affirm and encourage one another. In the process, your own faith will be strengthened as you discover that a faithful heart is one that is willing to share, stretch, and grow.

How the Study Works

Each week you will have six daily readings on one of the eight characteristics of a faithful heart. (Allow 10–15 minutes for each reading.) You will need to complete these readings prior to meeting with your group. This means that participants will need their books a week prior to the first group session so that they may complete the first week's readings. If you choose, you may hold an introductory session for this purpose (see pp. 9–12). Or simply distribute the books in advance with instructions for completing the first week's readings.

Day 1 of each week focuses on Mary and how she exemplified the given characteristic. Days 2–6 further develop and illustrate the characteristic through a variety of reflections, stories, and examples. Also at the beginning of each week you will note a practical challenge for the week, which is designed to help participants strengthen the characteristic in their lives. Participants may choose to complete the challenge anytime throughout the week and will have the opportunity to share their experiences at the beginning of the next group session. As you gather weekly with your group—whether you meet in a home, church, or other gathering place—you will have the option of a 60-minute or 90-minute session:

60-Minute Session

Opening (5 mins.)

Looking Into God's Word (15 mins.)

Discussing the Week's Reading (15 mins.)

Exploring Together (15 mins.)

Learning From a Faithful Example (5 mins.)

A Challenge (3 mins.)

Closing (2 mins.)

90-Minute Session

Opening (5 mins.)

Looking Into God's Word (20 mins.)

Discussing the Week's Reading (20 mins.)

Exploring Together (20 mins.)

Learning From a Faithful Example (10 mins.)

Journaling Prayer (10 mins.)

A Challenge (3 mins.)

Closing (2 mins.)

For ease of use throughout the sessions, words addressed to you, the leader, appear in **bold**.

In addition to prayer, Bible study, discussion, and a group activity ("Exploring Together"), each format option also includes the story of a contemporary woman who exemplifies a faithful heart ("Learning From a Faithful Example") and a challenge for the week. The 90-minute option extends some of the time allotments and includes time for journaling prayer. Of course, feel free to adapt these formats as you wish to meet the schedule and needs of your particular group.

As group leader, your role is more of facilitator than teacher. Your primary responsibility each week is to encourage participation and sharing by *all* group members. The more women are willing to interact and share with one another, the more they will be encouraged, strengthened, and challenged by the experience. Be willing to share first if necessary to get things going, but be careful not to monopolize the discussion, preventing others from sharing. Also be attentive to group members who may dominate discussion time, thanking them for their comments and inviting others to respond.

Be sure to respect group member's schedules by beginning and ending on time. If you see that a session is going to run long, make adjustments as necessary or get consensus from the group before exceeding the agreed upon ending time.

Prepare in advance for each session by reading the daily readings and the group session outline. Consider sharing leadership by inviting participants to take turns overseeing various aspects of the group session, such as leading prayer, directing the group activity, or reading the story of the contemporary example.

Above all, pray for your group. Pray for group members by name, and pray for the group sessions themselves. Prayer is the most important preparation you will do.

As you lead others to grow in the eight characteristics of a faithful heart, may you yourself discover the joy of a growing, faithful heart!

Introductory Session
(Optional)

Opening (5 mins.)

Welcome participants and open with prayer. Use the prayer provided below, or offer an original prayer:

Faithful God, we are grateful for the desire you have given us to cultivate a faithful heart—a heart that is growing in faithfulness to you, in love, and in joy. As we make a commitment to this eight-week journey, we eagerly anticipate what you will do in and through us. Thank you for all the faithful women who have gone before us and for all the faithful women who enrich our lives today. May we learn from one another and encourage one another as we seek to grow in faithfulness together. In Jesus' name. Amen.

Looking Into God's Word (10 mins.)

Our God, I am faithful to you with all my heart, . . .
I will sing and play music for you
with all that I am. (Psalm 108:1, CEV)

Some Bible translations use the word *steadfast* or *confident* in place of the word *faithful*. (If you wish, read Psalm 108:1 from several different Bible translations.) The idea is that the psalmist's faith or trust in God is fixed, constant, unchanging, steady. The psalmist is expressing loyalty to God, and the automatic or natural result of this confidence or trust in God is praise.

In this eight-week journey, we are seeking to cultivate or strengthen a faithful heart—a heart that is ever drawing closer to God and growing in faithfulness, love, and joy. The three are intertwined, for as we grow in faithfulness to God—as we experience God's love and faithfulness and our trust or confidence in God increases—so do our love and our joy. Praise is the automatic response of a faithful heart!

Sing a song or hymn of praise together now, expressing your trust and confidence in God. Or read in unison the words of a psalm of praise.

Discussing the Week's Reading (15 mins.)

Since you have not yet begun the weekly readings, read aloud the first three paragraphs of the introduction. Then discuss the following questions:

1. Prior to beginning our study together, how would you define or explain a "faithful heart"? *(Write words or phrases on a board or chart, if you like.)*
2. Why is it important to affirm and encourage one another as we seek to grow in faithfulness? Generally speaking, how have other women helped to encourage you toward growth in your faith walk?
3. Reflect silently for a moment on this statement: "A faithful heart is one that is willing to share, stretch, and grow." How willing are you to share, stretch, and grow? What obstacles, if any, threaten to hold you back, and what can you do to address them?

Exploring Together (10 mins.)

Have each woman briefly introduce herself, telling what she hopes to gain from this study.

Learning From a Faithful Example (5 mins.)

Read aloud the following:

Each of the eight sessions will include a brief portrait of a contemporary example of a faithful heart. For this introductory session, however, let us review a brief "portrait"of Mary from the Bible:

In the sixth month the angel Gabriel was sent by God to a town in Galilee called Nazareth, to a virgin engaged to a man whose name was Joseph, of the house of David. The virgin's name was Mary. And he came to her and said, "Greetings, favored one! The Lord is with you." But she was much perplexed by his words and pondered what sort of greeting this might be. The angel said to her, "Do not be afraid, Mary, for you have found favor with God. And now, you will conceive in your womb and bear a son, and you will name him Jesus. He will be great, and will be called the Son of the Most High, and the Lord God will give to him the throne of his ancestor David. He will reign over the house of Jacob forever, and of his kingdom there will be no end." Mary said to the angel, "How can this be, since I am a virgin?" The angel said to her, "The Holy Spirit will come upon you, and the power of the Most High will overshadow you; therefore the child to be born will be holy; he will be called Son of God. And now, your relative Elizabeth in her old age has also conceived a son; and this is the sixth month for her who was said to be barren. For nothing

11

will be impossible with God." Then Mary said, "Here am I, the servant of the Lord; let it be with me according to your word." Then the angel departed from her. (Luke 1:26-38)

Here we are introduced to Mary, who became one of the most prominent figures in the Bible and in the history of our faith. "Let it be with me according to your word," Mary said. As we continue this study over the next eight weeks, we will continue to examine the faithful heart of Mary.

A Challenge (3 mins.)

Hand out copies of the book *A Faithful Heart* and direct participants to p. 10. Introduce the challenge for Week 1, and instruct participants to complete the challenge and the daily readings before Session 1. Remind them of the date, time, and location of your next meeting.

Closing (2 mins.)

Close with a prayer or benediction, such as the following:

"Now to him who by the power at work within us is able to accomplish abundantly far more than all we can ask or imagine, to him be glory in the church and in Christ Jesus to all generations, forever and ever." Amen. (Ephesians 3:20-21)

Session

1

Passionate:
Beloved of God

Challenge for Week 1

This week, as you find yourself in an ordinary place or surrounding, practice seeing the presence of God. Recall what you see or sense, and journal about it or share the experience with a loved one or someone in the group.

Session 1
Passionate: Beloved of God

Suggested times are noted in parentheses. The first time is for a 60-minute session; the second time is for a 90-minute session. (If only one time is given, that time applies to both formats.) Note that Journaling Prayer is added to the 90-minute session.

Opening (5 mins.)

Welcome participants and open with prayer. Use the prayer provided below, or offer an original prayer:

Lord, surely your presence is in this place. Your word promises that you are always with us and that your Spirit lives within us. The evidence of your goodness is all around us. All we have to do is taste and see. You remind us in so many ways that we are your beloved. Open our eyes, ears, minds, and hearts so that we may experience you more fully. Teach us how to have a deep, abiding awareness of your presence, your goodness, and your love. We long to have a passionate faith. Amen.

Invite participants to briefly share their experiences with the challenge for Week 1.

Looking Into God's Word (15 mins. / 20 mins.)

Read aloud Romans 12:1-2:

> *I appeal to you therefore, brothers and sisters, by the mercies of God, to present your bodies as a living sacrifice, holy and acceptable to God, which is your spiritual worship. Do not be conformed to this world, but be transformed by the renewing of your minds, so that you may discern what is the will of God—what is good and acceptable and perfect.*

For most of us, this wording from the New Revised Standard Version is familiar. But what does it mean to present our bodies as a living sacrifice?

In the Old Testament, a sacrifice was an offering made to God as an atonement for sin, such as a slain animal, or an expression of thanksgiving, such as firstfruits. In either case, the one making the sacrifice relinquished all claim or right to the offering, giving it entirely for the honor of God.

Because Christ gave his life as the final and all-sufficient atonement for sin, we no longer are required to offer animal sacrifices. Instead, we offer our lives to God as an expression of thanksgiving for God's grace and mercy and goodness to us.

Hear the verses again from *The Message*:

> *So here's what I want you to do, God helping you: Take your everyday, ordinary life—your sleeping, eating, going-to-work, and walking-around life—and place it before God as an offering. Embracing what God does for you is the best thing you can do for [God]. (Romans 12:1-2)*

Offering our lives as a living sacrifice is dedicating every-thing we do every day without reserve to God. This requires us to be ever conscious of God's presence and activity, both in us and around us. Giving ourselves to God in this way is an act of worship. When we live this way, we think differently and respond to circumstances and people differently. We embrace all of life, even the difficult times, as holy moments in which God is fully and tangibly present with us.

Briefly Discuss:
- How does remembering and reflecting on the sacrificial system of the Old Testament, as well as Christ's sacrifice for us, impact your understanding of these verses?

Let's take a look at another key passage from the week.

Read aloud the following:

> So if you have been raised with Christ, seek the things that are above, where Christ is, seated at the right hand of God. Set your minds on things that are above, not on things that are on earth, for you have died, and your life is hidden with Christ in God. (Colossians 3:1-3)

Now listen to the same verses in *The Message*:

> So if you're serious about living this new resurrection life with Christ, act like it. Pursue the things over which Christ presides. Don't shuffle along, eyes to the ground, absorbed with the things right in front of you. Look up, and be alert to what is going on around Christ—that's where the action is. See things from his perspective. Your old life is dead. Your new life, which is your real life—even

17

though invisible to spectators—is with Christ in God. He
is your life. (Colossians 3:1-3)

One version instructs us to "set our minds on things that are above." The other words it differently, saying we are to keep alert and to see things from Christ's perspective. To "set" something requires deliberate action. Whether we are setting a watch, a table, a direction or course, a goal, or something else, we are intentional and focused. Can you imagine trying to set a watch without looking at it, or charting a course on a map while staring at the TV? To be effective or successful, we must fix our attention on the desired position or object or outcome. The same is true of living a passionate, faithful life in Christ. We must set or fix our minds on Christ, and when we do, we are able to see things—everything— through his eyes.

Briefly Discuss:
- Practically speaking, what does it mean to set your mind on Christ? What can help you to do this throughout the day?

Discussing the Week's Reading
(15 mins. / 20 mins.)

This week's readings have focused on what it means to have a passionate faith. When we have a passionate faith, we recognize the tangible presence of God every day. In other words, we deeply sense God's presence around us and within us at all times. When we are keenly aware of God's presence and experience God in our everyday lives, we see God's goodness all around us and seek God's will in our lives.

Choose from the following discussion questions:

1. Who have been the messengers of God's love to you this week? To whom have you been a messenger of God's love?
2. How have you seen the presence of God in an ordinary experience this week?
3. What are some practical ways we can practice seeing the presence of God every day?
4. Do you generally anticipate that you will experience the goodness of God? Why or why not? What can help you to cultivate this attitude?
5. When have you experienced the passionate, felt presence of God even when life is difficult, stressful, or painful?
6. Have you ever been "filled up" with a sense of the goodness of life and God? Where were you when this happened?
7. Are you someone who is often anxious and worried about many things? What's a reminder of God's goodness in your daily life that could help you do your very best to enjoy life?
8. How is your life an offering to God and to others? How have you taken (or how could you take) what you have in life and make something of it that is good and pleasing to yourself, to others, and to God?
9. How does seeing each day as holy change your perspective? What are some daily reminders of the holy in your life?
10. How might your daily chores, which are tedious, be "imbued with the presence of God"?

Exploring Together (15 mins. / 20 mins.)

Tell the group that they are going to be messenger's of God's love to one another. Each woman is to pair up with the woman on her right and spend 3–5 minutes affirming and encouraging her with words of love, appreciation, and respect. Keep time, and then have them switch roles for another 3–5 minutes. Suggest that they begin by concentrating on how God sees them and who they are in Christ. Then, if they know one another personally, they may move on to more personal affirmations. They also may choose to pray for one another during this time. (Note: If you have an odd number, assign a group of three and instruct two of the women to take turns affirming the other.)

Come back together as a group and discuss the experience:
- How did it feel hearing these words of love and affirmation?
- How does our attitude and perspective change when we see the love and encouragement others give us as "messages from God"—as evidence of God's presence and love?
- How would your life be different if you saw yourself as a messenger of God each day?

Learning From a Faithful Example (5 mins. / 10 mins.)

Read aloud the following portrait of Ruth Bell Graham, a contemporary example of a passionate faith.

Ruth Bell Graham (wife of evangelist Billy Graham)
(June 10, 1920 – June 14, 2007)

Ruth Bell Graham was born to medical missionaries living in China in 1920. She later met Billy at Wheaton College in

Illinois, and they were married in 1943. In addition to being the wife of one of the most famous preachers in modern history, Ruth also reared five children and authored or co-authored fourteen books. While preferring her role to be behind the scenes, Ruth joined her husband willingly in his ministry. Rev. Graham often turned to his wife for advice throughout his career, and she is credited with advising him to decline Hollywood movie deals in the 1940's and to refuse to run for national political office when he was approached by various Republicans to do so.[1]

Ruth's compassion for the people of Asia was evident as she encouraged and even accompanied her husband on visits to the People's Republic of China. Also a philanthropist, in 1966 Ruth founded the Ruth and Billy Graham Children's Health Center in Asheville, North Carolina. Her significant role in her husband's ministry was formally recognized when, in February of 1996, they were jointly awarded the Congressional Gold Medal, which is the highest expression of national appreciation given by Congress. Clearly, all of these accomplishments in her personal and professional life as well as her joint ministry with her husband could not have been possible without her passionate faith.

Journaling Prayer
(10 mins. – *90-minute session only*)

Each person will need a notebook or journal and a pen. Have everyone spread out in the room and find a comfortable posture for writing. Play a worshipful song appropriate to the week's theme, setting the CD player or MP3 player on repeat; or play several songs to fill the time. Instruct participants to write in their notebooks or journals in response to the following prayer prompt, allowing the Holy Spirit to lead their journaling. (Write the prayer prompt on a board or chart.)

God, when I deeply sense or experience your presence . . .

A Challenge (3 mins.)

Have participants turn to p. 36 in *A Faithful Heart* and review the challenge for Week 2.

Closing (2 mins.)

Close with a prayer or benediction, such as the following:

> *"Live in peace; and the God of love and peace will be with you. . . . The grace of the Lord Jesus Christ, the love of God, and the communion of the Holy Spirit be with all of you." Amen. (2 Corinthians 13:11, 13)*

[1] Laura Sessions Stepp, "Ruth Bell Graham, The Soul Mate of the Preacher," in *The Washington Post*, June 16, 2007; http://www.washingtonpost.com/wp-dyn/content/article/2007/06/15/AR2007061502363.html.

Session

2

Called:
Our Annunciation

Challenge for Week 2

What image or picture would you use to remind yourself that God is calling you? This week, choose or create a meaningful image to portray your calling. Place this somewhere you will see daily and remember your calling as God's beloved.

Session 2
Called: Our Annunciation

Suggested times are noted in parentheses. The first time is for a 60-minute session; the second time is for a 90-minute session. (If only one time is given, that time applies to both formats.) Note that Journaling Prayer is added to the 90-minute session.

Opening (5 mins.)

Welcome participants and open with prayer. Use the prayer provided below, or offer an original prayer:

Loving God, you have chosen us to be your children. You have called each of us to be in relationship with you as a trusting child relates to a loving parent. Yet not only do you call us to love you, you also call us to serve you by serving others and making a difference in the world—all for your glory. Help us to recognize the gifts and talents and abilities you have given each of us and the ways you are calling us to share them for the good of others. May we never forget that nothing is impossible with you, and that we can do all things through Christ who strengthens us. Amen.

Invite participants to briefly share their experiences with the challenge for Week 2.

Looking Into God's Word (15 mins. / 20 mins.)

Read aloud 1 Peter 2:9-10 from *The Message*:

> *But you are the ones chosen by God, chosen for the high calling of priestly work, chosen to be a holy people, God's instruments to do his work and speak out for him, to tell others of the night-and-day difference he made for you—from nothing to something, from rejected to accepted.*

Have you ever thought that you were chosen for priestly work? The Greek word used here for chosen is *eklektos*, which means "to select." It implies the idea of being favored or set apart as a favorite. We might think that these words are meant for those who are called to be set apart as pastors, missionaries, or others serving in full-time ministry. But actually they refer to anyone who is a follower of Jesus Christ.

You and I have been selected by God and set apart for ministry. We have been chosen for the holy calling of serving God by doing God's work and spreading God's message. Of course, how we do this differs from individual to individual as we use the unique gifts, abilities, and personalities God has given each of us to accomplish this holy calling, or purpose. In fact, most of us will fulfill this calling in a variety of different ways throughout our lifetimes as God brings us to new opportunities and challenges and "assignments."

Because the gifts God gives us help us to fulfill this holy calling of serving God, it may be helpful to quickly review the spiritual gifts mentioned in the Bible.

Ask three different individuals to read aloud the following passages:

Romans 12:6-8,
1 Corinthians 12:4-10
1 Corinthians 12:28

There are many excellent books and resources available that can help us to discover our spiritual gifts. Many of us already have an idea of the gifts we have been given. For our purposes this week, however, our focus is much broader, encompassing everything that makes us who God created us to be—including not only our gifts but also our talents, skills, interests, personalities, temperaments, and aptitudes. Some call this our "shape."

Briefly Discuss:
- How does it make you feel to know that you are favored and set apart for a holy calling?
- How has God "shaped" you to do God's work? Name 3–5 major aspects of your "shape"—these might include spiritual gifts, talents or abilities, interests, personality traits, or other characteristics that make you uniquely you. Quickly share the first 3–5 that come to mind. Here are a couple of examples:

  introverted, gift of encouragement, excellent writing skills, enjoy reading, extroverted, athletic, gift of teaching, enjoy working with youth

Discussing the Week's Reading
(15 mins. / 20 mins.)

This week's readings have focused on what it means to have a purpose-given life and to be called and gifted by God so that we can share who we are with others and make a difference in the world around us.

27

Choose from the following discussion questions:

1. What seems difficult or impossible for you right now? What are five things that you can do because of Christ?

2. Have you ever had an experience of God calling you? What was it like? Have you sensed God calling you in different ways and at different times in your life? How is God calling you at this point in your life's journey?

3. Why do we need daily reminders that God loves us, is with us, and is calling us to bear the message of Christ to the world? What serves (or could serve) as your daily reminder of this calling?

4. How would you express your life's meaning or story—your unique purpose or calling?

5. If God were to say to you, "Do anything that pleases you, and belong to me," what would this mean for you? What would you pursue that brings you enjoyment and gives God glory?

6. How is it possible to serve God and others in whatever we do? What difference would it make in your life and the lives of others if you had the attitude that you are serving God and your neighbor through whatever you do?

7. How can remembering our calling help us when we are in the midst of difficult circumstances or days?

8. What passion do you have that could be transformed into a ministry?

9. What would you call your life's work?

10. If we are defined by how we spend the majority of our time and how we treat others, how would you characterize your life? How would those who encounter you most often characterize your life?

Exploring Together (15 mins. / 20 mins.)

Choose from the following two activities. Option #1 is for groups whose members are well acquainted with one another. Option #2 is for groups whose members may be only newly acquainted.

<u>Option #1:</u> Affirming One Another's Uniqueness

Read aloud the following:

This week we looked at an old Jewish saying of Rabbi Zusya: "In the coming world, they will not ask me: 'Why were you not Moses?' They'll ask me: 'Why were you not Zusya?'" This saying points out the fact that we tend to compare ourselves to others and to imitate or emulate those we admire or esteem, yet God wants us to be uniquely ourselves. As strange as it may sound, sometimes it's easier for others to identify our gifts, strengths, and abilities than it is for us. In any case, others can be of great help in affirming the characteristics and strengths that make us who we are.

Write the following questions on a board or chart. Give each participant a sheet of paper and a pen or pencil, and ask her to quickly jot down brief answers to the questions on one side of the paper.

- What "stands out" about me or sets me apart from others? What makes me uniquely me?
- What are my strengths—in character and personality, as well as in gifts, talents, and abilities?

29

Once participants have recorded their own answers, have them move about the room, asking others to answer the questions about them. Have participants record the answers of others on the opposite side of the paper. Come back together and discuss the following:

- How were the comments of others the same as and/or different from your own responses?
- What did you learn from this exercise?

Option #2: Joining Self and Service

Read the following aloud:

This week we were introduced to Frederick Buechner's idea that true vocation joins self and service when "the place where your deep gladness and the world's deep hunger meet."[2]

Have participants break into pairs and take turns sharing what gives them "deep gladness"—what they are passionate about or what they enjoy doing more than anything. Then they are to brainstorm together how each of them might connect her passion with "the world's deep hunger." The idea is to list various ministries, areas of service, vocations, or even careers that would allow each of them to use their passion for the good of others and the glory of God. Ask them to be as specific or detailed as they can.

Learning From a Faithful Example
(5 mins. / 10 mins.)

Read aloud the following portrait of Leontine Kelly, a living example of someone who is called and gifted by God to make a difference in the world.

Leontine Kelly (first female African American bishop in The United Methodist Church)
(March 5, 1920 –)

As a high school social studies teacher, mother of four, and wife of a Methodist minister, Leontine Kelly's life was like that of many other women until her husband's death in 1969. It was then that Kelly received her own call to ordained ministry. After studying at Wesley Theological Seminary and Union Theological Seminary, she received her masters of divinity degree and was ordained. In 1983, Kelly became Assistant General Secretary in the area of Evangelism for the United Methodist General Board of Discipleship in Nashville, Tennessee. In 1984, she became the first African American woman to be elected bishop in her denomination—and holds the distinction of being the first African American woman to be elected bishop by any major religious denomination. She served as bishop of the California-Nevada Annual Conference and as president of the Western Jurisdiction College of Bishops, serving as the chief administrative officer and spiritual leader of more than 100,000 United Methodists in California and Nevada.

After retiring as bishop in 1988, Kelly served as a visiting professor of religion at many universities. As a spiritual and moral leader, Bishop Kelly has advanced the cause of justice in the United States and throughout the world. Throughout her career in ministry, she has been a social activist and role model, mentoring and counseling women in the ministry and ministering to AIDS victims. In 2000, Kelly was inducted in to the National Women's Hall of Fame. Also in 2000, her family established a scholarship fund in her name at United Methodist-related Africa University in Zimbabwe.

Journaling Prayer
(10 mins. – *90-minute session only*)

Each person will need a notebook or journal and a pen. Have everyone spread out in the room and find a comfortable posture for writing. Play a worshipful song appropriate to the week's theme, setting the CD player or MP3 player on repeat; or play several songs to fill the time. Instruct participants to write in their notebooks or journals in response to the following two prayer prompts, allowing the Holy Spirit to lead their journaling. (Write the prayer prompts on a board or chart.)

Lord, I feel most alive when . . .

At this point in my life's journey, God, I sense you calling me to . . .

A Challenge (3 mins.)

Have participants turn to p. 66 in *A Faithful Heart* and review the challenge for Week 3.

Closing (2 mins.)

Close with a prayer or benediction, such as the following:

May the God of peace himself sanctify you entirely; and may your spirit and soul and body be kept sound and blameless at the coming of our Lord Jesus Christ. The one who calls you is faithful, and he will do this. (1 Thessalonians 5:23-24)

---

[2] Frederick Buechner, *Wishful Thinking: A Seeker's ABC* (HarperSanFrancisco, 1993); p. 119.

Session

3

Holy:
Practicing Healthy Habits

Challenge for Week 3

Take time this week to practice a holy, healthy habit. This might be practicing a breath prayer while taking a walk in your neighborhood. Or you might work on balancing your Spiritual Pyramid in one or more areas this week, setting short- and long-term goals for yourself.

Session 3
Holy: Practicing Healthy Habits

Suggested times are noted in parentheses. The first time is for a 60-minute session; the second time is for a 90-minute session. (If only one time is given, that time applies to both formats.) Note that Journaling Prayer is added to the 90-minute session.

Opening (5 mins.)

Welcome participants and open with prayer. Use the prayer provided below, or offer an original prayer:

Most Holy God, you call us to a life of holy devotion and healthy habits. Your own Son, Jesus, spent many hours in private prayer and was intimately familiar with the Scriptures. We know that he observed the sabbath and holy days, went to the Temple regularly, and studied and taught in the synagogue. We also know that he took care of his physical body, walking great distances with his disciples and eating according to the strict dietary laws of Judaism. Although we cannot be perfect as Jesus was and attain a perfectly balanced spiritual life, we can strive for greater balance in our spiritual lives and thus increase the overall welfare of our spirits. Give us the desire, discipline, and determination to practice holy, healthy habits so that we may become more like Jesus. Amen.

Invite participants to briefly share their experiences with the challenge for Week 3.

Looking Into God's Word (15 mins. / 20 mins.)

Read aloud the following verses:

> *One final word, friends. We ask you—urge is more like it—that you keep on doing what we told you to do to please God, not in a dogged religious plod, but in a living, spirited dance. You know the guidelines we laid out for you from the Master Jesus. God wants you to live a pure life. . . . Learn to appreciate and give dignity to your body, not abusing it, as is so common among those who know nothing of God. . . . God hasn't invited us into a disorderly, unkempt life but into something holy and beautiful—as beautiful on the inside as the outside.* (1 Thessalonians 4:1-3a, 4-5, 7, The Message)

In verse 3 we are told that God wants us to live a pure life. The New Revised Standard Version puts it this way: "For this is the will of God, your sanctification." The Greek word for sanctification is *hagiasmos*, which comes from the verb *hagiazó*, meaning "to make holy, purify, or consecrate." To consecrate something is to make or declare it sacred or holy. The Bible tells us that only God is holy, and therefore only God can make something holy. Yet these verses plainly show that we also play a role in the process. The apostle Paul urges us to live in a way that pleases God—to live a pure life in every way.

The point is clear: We have a choice. We can choose to live a pure life or to live an impure life. Though it is God who gives us the strength and ability to make right, healthy choices and thus to live a pure life, we first must choose purity and then, by faith, step out to pursue it. As we do, God steps in to empower us.

Have someone read aloud Philippians 2:12.

This verse tells us that God works in us to help us work out our salvation. The same thing can be said of our sanctification. In fact, the Greek word for salvation means health and wholeness. God works in us to help us work out the process of becoming completely whole—like Christ. This is the process of sanctification.

Knowing this should encourage us. Without this assurance, the command to love God with all our heart, soul, and strength is daunting, to say the least. But as Jesus said, "What is impossible for mortals is possible for God" (Luke 18:27). As we take steps to practice healthy, holy habits, God will step in to help us. God's objective is to make us holy— to conform us into the image of Christ. And we can be confident that God will be faithful to complete the process.

Have someone read aloud Philippians 1:6.

Briefly Discuss:
- When it comes to trying to live a holy, healthy life, what discourages you?
- How does understanding God's part in our sanctification—to enable and empower—give you encouragement for your part—to practice holy, healthy habits?

Discussing the Week's Reading
(15 mins. / 20 mins.)

This week's readings have focused on practicing holy, healthy habits.

Choose from the following discussion questions:

1. Would you describe yourself as a "ponderer," like Mary? Why or why not? Why is pondering—thinking deeply about, contemplating, and meditating on what God is saying to us and doing through us—important to our spiritual growth?

2. What helps you to focus your prayers? Have you ever used prayer beads? If so, share how this practice has helped to focus your prayers.

3. How balanced is your spiritual life? Is there an area of the Spiritual Pyramid that you need to give more time and attention (personal Bible study/prayer, small-group discipleship, service in the church, worship, service and outreach, retreats)?

4. What are your practices in reading Scripture? What obstacles or challenges do you face when trying to set aside time for Bible study and prayer, and how do you address them?

5. Have you ever had an experience of a story or passage from the Bible "falling inside" your heart during a difficult time? Share as you are willing.

6. In what area of your life do you need "strength training"? It might be physical, mental, spiritual, or even emotional. What's one thing you could do to better care for yourself as you face the marathon of your life?

7. What's your most common form of prayer (thanksgiving, praise, intercession for others, supplication for personal needs, confession, etc.)? In other words, which form of prayer do you devote more time to? Which do you need or want to cultivate more intentionally?

8. What is breath prayer, and what are some of its benefits? What phrase would you choose for a breath prayer? When might you use breath prayer?

Exploring Together (15 mins. / 20 mins.)

Choose one of the following activities.

<u>Option #1:</u> Prayer Beads

Make prayer beads together. Prayer beads can be fancy or simple. In advance of the group session, go to a craft or bead store to find different beads to represent specific prayer prompts. (See the illustration on p. 40 for an example.) You also will want to purchase wire or elastic for stringing the beads.

As you begin, explain to participants that prayer beads are not bracelets. The beads should just slip over the fingers so that they circle the outer hand and palm; they are not to be worn as a bracelet on one's wrist. They are not jewelry but an aid to prayer.

Designate specific beads for each of the prayer prompts, or allow the women to choose their own. Talk about how to use the prayer beads as you string them together. The concept is to touch each bead as you pray on the topic it represents, moving around the circle in a focused pattern of prayer.

God
Prayers of thanksgiving and praise to God

Pray for the world

Self
Prayers for self

Worries
Tell your worries to God & leave them there

Three special concerns

Silence
Be silent & listen for God

Desert of Faith
What are you working on in your faith?

Those you love
and those you have trouble loving

Night & Day
What are you struggling with in your life? Offer to God.

Your Special Concern

Option #2: Sharing Holy, Healthy Habits

Read aloud the following excerpt from *A Faithful Heart*:

> I don't think we share our holy, healthy habits with each other enough; as a result, we don't get ideas from each other about how to incorporate them into our lives. Each of us needs to find a rhythm of practicing our holy, healthy habits, depending upon the circumstances of our lives. Circumstances of life will get in the way from time to time but far less so if we carve out the rhythm that works for us. (p. 70)

Invite the women to take turns sharing their holy, healthy habits with one another. If they are not sure where to begin, remind them of the author's examples on pp. 67–70 of *A Faithful Heart*. Encourage them to mention habits related to their physical, spiritual, emotional, and mental "fitness" or well-being. Have them write down any new ideas they would like to try.

Learning From a Faithful Example
(5 mins. / 10 mins.)

Read aloud the following portrait of Mary Lou Retton, a faithful example of someone who practices healthy habits.

Mary Lou Retton (Olympic gymnast)
(January 24, 1968 –)

Mary Lou Retton was born the youngest of five children in Fairmont, West Virginia, in 1968. But at the age of sixteen, Mary Lou became an international star when she won the All Around Gold Medal in women's gymnastics at the 1984 Olympic Games in Los Angeles, becoming the first American woman ever to win a gold medal in the sport of gymnastics. Her other victories include being the only woman to win three American Cups (1983–85), the All Around title and both the 1984 National Championships and Olympic Trials, as well as many other titles. Dubbed "America's Sweetheart" by the media, Retton was adored by fans. She even became the first woman athlete to ever appear on the front of a Wheaties cereal box.

After retiring from the sport in 1986 to pursue her education, Retton utilized her celebrity to become a motivational speaker and writer. In 2000, she published her first book, *Mary Lou Retton's Gateways to Happiness: Seven Ways to a More Peaceful, More Prosperous, More Satisfying Life*. Continuing to touch the lives of millions through teaching about health and happiness, Retton travels the world as a "Fitness Ambassador," promoting the benefits of proper nutrition and regular exercise. Crediting her faith in God as a major source of her happiness and stamina, Mary Lou has learned the importance of maintaining balance according to "the Lord's timeline" for her life—through his guidance and direction.[3]

41

Journaling Prayer
(10 mins. – *90-minute session only*)

Each person will need a notebook or journal and a pen. Have everyone spread out in the room and find a comfortable posture for writing. Play a worshipful song appropriate to the week's theme, setting the CD player or MP3 player on repeat; or play several songs to fill the time. Instruct participants to write in their notebooks or journals in response to the following prayer prompt, allowing the Holy Spirit to lead their journaling. (Write the prayer prompt on a board or chart.)

Lord, you have revealed to me that one of the areas of my spiritual life that currently is out of balance is . . .

A Challenge (3 mins.)

Have participants turn to p. 96 in *A Faithful Heart* and review the challenge for Week 4.

Closing (2 mins.)

Close with a prayer or benediction, such as the following:

Beloved, build yourselves up on your most holy faith; pray in the Holy Spirit; keep yourselves in the love of God; look forward to the mercy of our Lord Jesus Christ that leads to eternal life. . . . Now to him who is able to keep you from falling, and to make you stand without blemish in the presence of his glory with rejoicing, to the only God our Savior, through Jesus Christ our Lord, be glory, majesty, power, and authority, before all time and now and forever. Amen. (Jude 1:20-21, 24-25)

---

[3] Christin Ditchfield, "Mary Lou Retton: Role Model, Mother, Baptist," in *Baptist Standard,* January 19, 2000; http://www.baptiststandard.com/2000/1_19/pages/retton.html.

Session

4

Equipped:
A Community of Faith

Challenge for Week 4

Consider how you have experienced true community throughout different times in your life. How can you, likewise, offer true community to others? Look for opportunities this week to extend an invitation to someone who might be hungry for community.

Session 4
Equipped: A Community of Faith

Suggested times are noted in parentheses. The first time is for a 60-minute session; the second time is for a 90-minute session. (If only one time is given, that time applies to both formats.) Note that Journaling Prayer is added to the 90-minute session.

Opening (5 mins.)

Welcome participants and open with prayer. Use the prayer provided below, or offer an original prayer:

God who calls us into community, you designed us for relationship—relationship with you and with others. The church was your idea, established by your Son. He chose twelve disciples to be his inner circle—his small group—and many more followers traveled with him, sharing life and ministry together. Jesus knew that we need each other if we are to grow in our understanding of the Scriptures, learn to pray with and for one another, support one another, and hold one another accountable for our practices and growth. He knew that we must build one another up in love if we are to be successful in meeting the needs of a hurting world and in spreading the good news. Teach us how to be a true community—a community that not only rejoices together but also suffers together, a community that welcomes and accepts all, a community that reaches beyond itself to join you where you are working in the world. And God, when there is conflict, as there inevitably will be, may we choose to remain in relationship and to be the change we want to see in the church. All this we ask for your glory and your renown. Amen.

Invite participants to briefly share their experiences with the challenge for Week 4.

Looking Into God's Word (15 mins. / 20 mins.)

Read aloud the following:

> *For I am longing to see you so that I may share with you some spiritual gift to strengthen you—or rather so that we may be mutually encouraged by each other's faith, both yours and mine. (Romans 1:11-12)*

In these verses written by the apostle Paul, we find two of the purposes of meeting together in Christian community: 1) strengthening or assisting one another with our spiritual gifts, and 2) encouraging one another's faith. But perhaps the overarching purpose or reason for participating in a faith community is found in Ephesians 4:15-16.

Read the verses aloud, or have someone else read them.

> *Speaking the truth in love, we must grow up in every way into him who is the head, into Christ, from whom the whole body, joined and knit together by every ligament with which it is equipped, as each part is working properly, promotes the body's growth in building itself up in love. (Ephesians 4:15-16)*

Only in community are we able to "grow up in every way . . . into Christ"—to be conformed to the image of Christ. Think of a child trying to grow up on his or her own, apart from a family, and compare that child to one who is cared for, nurtured, and even disciplined by a loving, devoted family. Or contrast a new couple trying to raise young children without the help or support of extended family, neighbors, or friends with a couple who has the encouragement and help of a large family and a supportive community of friends and neighbors. The old African proverb "It takes a village to raise a child" has application to the faith community as well. It takes a community of faith to develop a disciple of Christ.

As we encourage and assist one another's growth in Christ, the whole body—whether it be the church or some sub-set or group within the church—is built up in love. As we work together, each one doing what he or she has been equipped to do, we spread God's message of love by both word and deed.

Have someone read aloud John 13:35.

The world recognizes that we are followers of Jesus by our love for one another—and our love for the world. Being part of a faith community both equips and identifies us as disciples of Jesus Christ.

One of the greatest challenges we face—and potentially the most destructive—is division within the faith community. Nothing stunts our spiritual growth or destroys our witness more readily than conflict or division within a faith community. Unfortunately, we all know how rampant it is— within groups, churches, and even denominations. Paul's words to the Christians in Ephesus and Philippi centuries ago give us wise instruction today as well:

Lead a life worthy of the calling to which [we] have been called, with all humility and gentleness, with patience, bearing with one another in love, making every effort to maintain the unity of the Spirit in the bond of peace. (Ephesians 4:1b-3)

Let each of you look not to your own interests, but to the interests of others. Let the same mind be in you that was in Christ Jesus. (Philippians 2:4-5)

Of course, Paul was not instructing these Christians to deviate from the truth. Rather, as we heard in the passage read earlier, he told them to "speak the truth in love" (Ephesians 4:15), always remaining humble and gentle and peace-seeking. He told them to think more about the other person than they did about themselves, and to think—and therefore speak—like Christ.

Briefly Discuss:
- Based on the passages we have looked at today, would you say that your faith community is promoting healthy growth among its members and building up the body in love? Why or why not?
- How would things be different—in your small group, your church, your denomination, and the larger Christian community—if we followed Paul's instructions?

Discussing the Week's Reading (15 mins. / 20 mins.)

This week's readings have focused on being part of a faith community in order to grow in our faith and become more like Christ, supporting and encouraging one another along the way.

48

Choose from the following discussion questions:

1. How has being part of a small group within a faith community enriched your life and faith?
2. What do you believe is the most critical aspect of a healthy small group?
3. How has a faith-based small group helped you to articulate and/or work through questions, beliefs, or circumstances in the past?
4. What are some of the challenges of being in a small group, and how can we address these challenges?
5. What makes it difficult to stay in relationship with those who differ from you about Scripture or some aspect of the Christian faith? How can we stay in relationship when there is disagreement or conflict, and what does this "look like"?
6. What experiences have you had personally with others who disagreed with you about deep spiritual matters? What happened? How have you grown in faith and spiritual maturity by staying in relationship with those individuals?
7. Who is the most unlikely person that your faith community has brought into your life? What have you learned from that person about life and faith?
8. Why is it important to widen your circle of acquaintances so that your uniqueness is enhanced by others? How can your faith community encourage this kind of attitude?
9. Have you ever experienced the desire for true community? Did you find it, and if so, how? How do you purposefully extend true community to others?
10. What kind of church do you want for your children or grandchildren—the next generation? What can you do to help make it that way? How can you be the "change you wish to see"?

Exploring Together (15 mins. / 20 mins.)

Read the following aloud:

We are the church to those outside its walls. For some, we're the only representation of "church" they may have. We need to ask ourselves, *What kind of church are we presenting to others?*

Brainstorm together positive, Christ-like ways that you can "take the church" with you into the world where you live, work, and relate to others. Choose one of these ideas to champion as a group, and write an action plan for putting it into action in the next four weeks.

Learning From a Faithful Example
(5 mins. / 10 mins.)

Read aloud the following portrait of Rosalynn Carter, a faithful example of someone who is equipped for ministry in the world.

Rosalynn Carter (wife of former President Jimmy Carter) *(August 18, 1927 –)*

While First Lady of the United States of America from 1977–1981, Rosalynn Carter is a political activist whose husband, the President, often consulted her and sought her advice on his domestic and foreign affairs decisions and speeches. Throughout her husband's presidency, they maintained a Wednesday business lunch in the Oval Office to discuss Administration policy on issues or legislative matters of concern to her. And in 1979, during her tenure, the federal government more formally recognized the role of First Lady as a bona fide federal position.[4]

Rosalynn Carter assumed an active role in the Administration's response and initiative on behalf of several domestic and foreign issues, the most significant being her work as the Active Honorary Chair of the President's Commission on Mental Health, which began in February of 1977. Mrs. Carter oversaw an advisory board of commissioners composed of social workers, medical experts, lobbyists, and psychiatrists, suggesting that a 1963 act be overhauled to strengthen services and create changes to health insurance coverage to support the most chronically mentally ill and advocating a bill of rights protecting the mentally ill from discrimination. Mrs. Carter testified on the Commission's behalf before the Senate Subcommittee on Health in May of 1979, and it was passed in September 1980.

Mrs. Carter is also involved with Habitat for Humanity, an organization of volunteers who build homes for the needy, and Project Interconnections, a nonprofit partnership to provide housing for the mentally ill who are homeless. Equipped with a community of support and a drive for justice, Mrs. Carter has brought true change to the lives of many in need.

Journaling Prayer
(10 mins. – *90-minute session only*)

Each person will need a notebook or journal and a pen. Have everyone spread out in the room and find a comfortable posture for writing. Play a worshipful song appropriate to the week's theme, setting the CD player or MP3 player on repeat; or play several songs to fill the time. Instruct participants to write in their notebooks or journals in response to the following two prayer prompts, allowing the Holy Spirit to lead their journaling. (Write the prayer prompts on a board or chart.)

Lord, I desire to experience true community. For me, this means . . .

You are calling me to extend true community to others by . . .

A Challenge (3 mins.)

Have participants turn to p. 126 in *A Faithful Heart* and review the challenge for Week 5.

Closing (2 mins.)

Close with a prayer or benediction, such as the following:

> *Now may our God and Father himself and our Lord Jesus direct our way to you. And may the Lord make you increase and abound in love for one another and for all, just as we abound in love for you. And may he so strengthen your hearts in holiness that you may be blameless before our God and Father at the coming of our Lord Jesus with all his saints. (1 Thessalonians 3:11-13)*

[4] From the National First Ladies' Library, "First Lady Biography: Rosalynn Carter"; http://www.firstladies.org/biographies/firstladies.aspx?biography=40.

5

Joyful:
An Evangelistic Heart

Challenge for Week 5

Consider how your own evangelistic heart has grown and developed through the years. Who has "scattered joy" in your life? Whose contagious joy caused you to grow in your faith? If you are able, contact one of these people this week. Write a note or send an e-mail, tweet, or text. Let them know you are grateful for their evangelistic heart.

Session 5
Joyful: An Evangelistic Heart

Suggested times are noted in parentheses. The first time is for a 60-minute session; the second time is for a 90-minute session. (If only one time is given, that time applies to both formats.) Note that Journaling Prayer is added to the 90-minute session.

Opening (5 mins.)

Welcome participants and open with prayer. Use the prayer provided below, or offer an original prayer:

God, you are the giver of joy, and you have filled us with joy because of the good news of Jesus Christ. We pray that this joy so "bubbles up" in our lives that we can't help sharing it with others. Give us eyes to see what you are doing in our lives and hearts that are so grateful that we are eager to share your love and grace with others. May the joy of our faith be so contagious that others want what we have. We also acknowledge, God, that although we never lose the abiding joy of Christ, sometimes our hearts are sad and broken—broken for those who suffer physically, emotionally, spiritually, and in many other ways. Make us sensitive to the ways you are calling us to reach out to others in love through our words and our actions. In Jesus' name. Amen.

Invite participants to briefly share their experiences with the challenge for Week 5.

Looking Into God's Word (15 mins. / 20 mins.)

Read aloud the following:

> *You are the light of the world. A city built on a hill cannot be hid. No one after lighting a lamp puts it under the bushel basket, but on the lampstand, and it gives light to all in the house. In the same way, let your light shine before others, so that they may see your good works and give glory to your Father in heaven. (Matthew 5:14-16)*

If you were to define evangelism according to these verses alone, how would you explain it?

Allow for brief discussion.

What does it mean to "let your light shine before others"?

Allow for brief discussion.

Lighting a lamp and putting it on a lampstand is an action. Although this metaphor is not limited to non-verbal actions, Jesus refers specifically in verse 16 to "good works." The Greek word used for works is *ergon*, meaning "act, deed, or labor." Letting our light shine involves doing good works that glorify God. Evangelism is love in action.

Evangelism is also verbal.

Read aloud the following passage:

Jesus sent his twelve harvest hands out with this charge: "Don't begin by traveling to some far-off place to convert unbelievers. And don't try to be dramatic by tackling some public enemy. Go to the lost, confused people right here in the neighborhood. Tell them that the kingdom is here. Bring health to the sick. Raise the dead. Touch the untouchables. Kick out the demons. You have been treated generously, so live generously. (Matthew 10:5-6, The Message*)*

Here, the first instruction Jesus gave to the disciples was to tell others the good news. Though the other actions he mentioned were important and even miraculous, even more important was telling others about Jesus.

Good deeds apart from the good news of Jesus Christ are empty, for it is only by the power of the gospel and of Christ working in and through us that real transformation can take place in others. At times the words precede the actions, and at other times the actions precede the words. In fact, often it is our actions that cause others to inquire about our motivation, which gives us an opportunity to share our faith. The apostle Peter acknowledged this when he wrote these words.

Have someone read aloud 1 Peter 3:15.

Now hear the same verse from *The Message*:

Be ready to speak up and tell anyone who asks why you're living the way you are, and always with the utmost courtesy. (1 Peter 3:15)

57

So, evangelism involves both words and actions. One without the other is incomplete. Without words that point to Jesus Christ—whether spoken immediately or at a later time—our good deeds are ineffective in bringing about lasting change in people's hearts and lives. May we never forget that it is the message of Jesus Christ that sets Christian evangelism apart from humanitarian aid.

Likewise, without good deeds that show the love of Christ in action, our words are hollow and empty. James wrote,

> If a brother or sister is naked and lacks daily food, and one of you says to them, "Go in peace; keep warm and eat your fill," and yet you do not supply their bodily needs, what is the good of that? So faith by itself, if it has no works, is dead. (James 2:15-17)

Verse 17 in *The Message* puts it this way:

> Isn't it obvious that God-talk without God-acts is outrageous nonsense?

In other words, telling others of Christ's love without showing Christ's love is useless. The love of Christ compels us to reach out in tangible, practical ways to help others. True evangelism is sharing the love of Christ through both our words and our actions.

Briefly Discuss:
- Do you agree that effective evangelism requires both words and actions? Why or why not?
- What are some effective evangelism efforts that you have participated in or observed?

Discussing the Week's Reading
(15 mins. / 20 mins.)

This week's readings have focused on what it means to have an evangelistic heart—a heart that is passionate for people in need and joyful because of what God is doing in her life, causing her to reach out to others.

Choose from the following discussion questions:

1. Have you ever had such good news that you couldn't wait to tell your mother, sister, friend, coworker, the woman on the bus, *anyone* because it was so wonderful? What was it, and who did you tell?

2. Have you ever had an experience when someone asked you why you cared or why you do what you do in such a caring way? How did you respond?

3. Have you ever seen the presence of God shining through someone else as she or he went about doing a job, performing some task, or doing something that really wasn't "religious work" but nevertheless revealed the light of God in her or his life?

4. Sometimes a deep interest or excitement about learning and growing in our faith causes us to connect with people—whether we know them or not—about spiritual matters. To whom do you talk about God in your day to day life?

5. How would you define evangelism? What are some ways we can share the love and grace of Jesus to those outside the church through words and actions?

6. What metaphor could you use to tell your story of faith to others? How would you tell it?

7. Now think about someone in your life you'd like to share the love and grace of Jesus with. What is that person's metaphor? How could you tell Jesus' story through that person's metaphor?
8. How is God enlarging and stretching your heart? Who does your heart break for?
9. How have you experienced joy in another's faith that you found contagious? How is God calling you to "scatter joy"?

Exploring Together (15 mins. / 20 mins.)

Read aloud the following excerpt from *A Faithful Heart*:

An evangelistic heart is interested in how other people experience and express their faith in God, and the best way to do that is to talk to them about it. That means the subject of God seems to come up in conversations naturally, regardless of whether or not the person goes to your church, or how well you know the person, or even if they would describe themselves as Christian. Just as it's natural to talk about the weather, which is everywhere and constantly impacting us, why wouldn't we talk about God, who is everywhere, all the time? (p. 128)

Divide into small groups of 3–4 and have the women share what God is currently doing in their lives—or have them answer this question: "What in your relationship with God or your faith journey are you excited about right now?" Tell them to discuss ways they can share the light of God and their excitement about their faith with others in their daily lives—whether they be family members, neighbors

or friends, co-workers, or strangers they meet while standing in line.

Learning From a Faithful Example
(5 mins. / 10 mins.)

Read aloud the following portrait of Lottie Moon, a faithful example of an evangelistic heart.

Lottie Moon (Baptist missionary to China)
(December 12, 1840 – December 24, 1912)

> *"I would I had a thousand lives that I might give them to . . . China!"*[5]

> — *Lottie Moon*
> *Zhenjiang, China*
> *August 27, 1888*

At the age of thirty-two, turning down a marriage proposal and leaving her job, home, and family, Lottie Moon followed God's leading and set sail for China. There, she spent the next thirty-nine years serving God and the Chinese people. Her vision reached beyond the people of China to her fellow Christians in the United States as she wrote letters home detailing the struggle of so few missionaries to share the gospel with so many. In her letters, she urged more workers to come and for her denomination, the Southern Baptist Convention, to support them prayerfully and financially.

In 1888, Lottie wrote a letter that was printed in the *Foreign Mission Journal*, pleading for reinforcements. Later that year, the first Christmas offering provided three additional missionaries. Lottie's letter is credited as providing the impetus for the creation of a Southern Baptist offering to support international missions, which later became the Lottie Moon Christmas Offering® of the International Mission Board, an annual offering of which all proceeds go to supporting Southern Baptist missionaries who, like Lottie, share the gospel overseas. In 2009, despite the sluggish economy, the Christmas Offering was $148.9 million, the third-largest Lottie Moon offering in history.[6]

Even Lottie's death rings true of her evangelistic heart for others. In 1912, during a time of famine in China, Lottie silently starved, giving all her food and money to famine relief. This was the ultimate sign of her love: giving her life for others. She died on Christmas Eve, on a ship bound for the United States.

Journaling Prayer
(10 mins. – *90-minute session only*)

Each person will need a notebook or journal and a pen. Have everyone spread out in the room and find a comfortable posture for writing. Play a worshipful song appropriate to the week's theme, setting the CD player or MP3 player on repeat; or play several songs to fill the time. Instruct participants to write in their notebooks or journals in response to the following two prayer prompts, allowing the Holy Spirit to lead their journaling. (Write the prayer prompts on a board or chart.)

God, I feel you are enlarging and stretching my heart, giving me an evangelistic heart for . . .

I want to . . .

A Challenge (3 mins.)

Have participants turn to p. 154 in *A Faithful Heart* and review the challenge for Week 6. (Look ahead to p. 71; see note in "Exploring Together" for options for group participation on the challenge.)

Closing (2 mins.)

Close with a prayer or benediction, such as the following:

Now may our Lord Jesus Christ himself and God our Father, who loved us and through grace gave us eternal comfort and good hope, comfort your hearts and strengthen them in every good work and word. (2 Thessalonians 2:16-17)

[5] International Mission Board, "Quoteables: Lottie Herself"; http://www.imb.org/main/give/page.asp?StoryID=5530&LanguageID=1709.
[6] Don Graham, "$148.9M Is 3rd-Largest Lottie Moon Offering," in *Baptist Press*, June 4, 2010; http://www.bpnews.net/bpnews.asp?id=33071.

Loving:
A World in Our Eyes

Challenge for Week 6

On your own or as a group, find an organization (local or international) that needs your help. Ideas might be to write letters of encouragement to women who are in recovery from domestic violence or drug abuse, send care packages to children in Third World countries, volunteer locally, or contact your church for additional ideas about organizations they already support.

Session 6
Loving: A World in Our Eyes

Suggested times are noted in parentheses. The first time is for a 60-minute session; the second time is for a 90-minute session. (If only one time is given, that time applies to both formats.) Note that Journaling Prayer is added to the 90-minute session.

Opening (5 mins.)

Welcome participants and open with prayer. Use the prayer provided below, or offer an original prayer:

Loving God, you so loved the world that you gave your only Son for us. You call us to love the world with the same kind of sacrificial love. Help us to reach out with your love and grace to those both near and far away, so that others may know you, experience your justice and peace, and live in an environment that provides all the good things you created. Make us keenly aware of the world's great needs, and fill us with passion and determination to respond. May we be diligent in prayer for those in need and faithful in our efforts not only to provide relief and assistance, but also to work for justice and lasting change. In Jesus' name. Amen.

Invite participants to briefly share their experiences with the challenge for Week 6.

Looking Into God's Word (15 mins. / 20 mins.)

Read the following aloud:

To have the world in our eye is to see the world's needs and reach out in love to meet them. God's desire is that we love the world as God loves the world. The prophet Micah expressed it this way:

> *He has told you, O mortal, what is good; and what does the LORD require of you but to do justice, and to love kindness, and to walk humbly with your God? (Micah 6:8)*

The Hebrew word for justice in this verse is *mishpat*, which means the act of deciding a case by making a right or moral judgment. In other words, justice is setting things right. God calls us not only to love others but also to work for justice on their behalf—to defend their cause so that things may be set right.

The Hebrew word for kindness used here is *checed*, which connotes goodness, faithfulness, lovingkindness, and mercy. Those who are proud can offer neither *mishpat* nor *checed*— neither justice nor kindness—which is why we are told to walk humbly with our God. Only an attitude of humility allows us to love as selflessly as Jesus loved, working for justice and serving others with kindness.

Briefly Discuss:
- Why do you think humility is a prerequisite for justice and kindness?

The prophet Isaiah wrote to people who thought they were humbly seeking to worship and serve God, yet their hearts

68

were not right, and therefore their actions were unacceptable to God. They fasted and sat in sackcloth and ashes while taking advantage of their workers and arguing among themselves. Isaiah described to them the kind of humility God desires. Listen to this rendering from *The Message*:

> *This is the kind of fast day I'm after: to break the chains of injustice, get rid of exploitation in the workplace, free the oppressed, cancel debts. What I'm interested in seeing you do is: sharing your food with the hungry, inviting the homeless poor into your homes, putting clothes on the shivering ill-clad, being available to your own families. Do this and the lights will turn on, and your lives will turn around at once. Your righteousness will pave your way. (Isaiah 58:6-8)*

According to Isaiah, doing what is right and just on behalf of others is the way to please God and live a righteous life. This is a recurring theme in the prophet's writings. At the beginning of the Book of Isaiah, we find a similar exhortation.

Have someone read aloud Isaiah 1:17.

These words are in keeping with words Isaiah wrote about the work of the Messiah. Jesus read these words to the people in the synagogue in Nazareth and proclaimed that he had fulfilled the words in their hearing:

> *When [Jesus] came to Nazareth. . . . he stood up to read, and the scroll of the prophet Isaiah was given to him. He unrolled the scroll and found the place where it was written: "The Spirit of the Lord is upon me, because he has anointed me to bring good news to the poor. He has sent*

*me to proclaim release to the captives and recovery of sight
to the blind, to let the oppressed go free, to proclaim the
year of the Lord's favor." (Luke 4:16-19)*

Jesus came not only to save the world for eternity, but also to
bring justice and mercy for the here and now. As his followers, it is our responsibility to take up the cause and continue
the work in his name. Walking as Jesus walked and loving as
Jesus loved means working for justice and mercy in a hurting world.

Briefly Discuss:
- How would the church today be different if we truly
  loved the world as Jesus does?

Discussing the Week's Reading
(15 mins. / 20 mins.)

This week's readings have focused on loving the world as
intensely as Jesus does.

Choose from the following discussion questions:
1. When you were a teenager, what issues of justice
   were you passionate about? Do you have a sense of
   justice now toward a group of people, especially
   other than your own, that sparks passion in your
   soul? Why or why not?
2. What part of the world grabs your heart as you see it
   groaning in pain and suffering? How do you pray
   for the world?
3. What specific issues and needs of people in other
   parts of the world do you feel called to pray for? What
   does it feel like to pray for people you don't know?
   How do you feel praying for those experiencing

extreme adversity when there might not be much you can do about it?

4. Have you ever been on a mission trip? What was it like? How do you feel about that part of the world as a result of going there and being with people through mission?

5. Are you more prone to offer mercy or to work for justice? What is the difference between the two—between acts of charity and acts seeking lasting change?

6. Do you think "ecology is part of theology"? Do you see caring for creation as part of your Christian discipleship? Why or why not?

7. What practices might you add to your life to care for God's creation?

Exploring Together (15 mins. / 20 mins.)

Discuss nations/people groups in other parts of the world that are suffering. Choose one of these nations/groups and discuss ways that you can reach out in love to these people through prayer as well as through specific actions you might take, whether individually or collectively. Choose one action you can take as a group and make plans to carry it out. Pray together for this part of the world that is in God's eye. (Note: You may choose to carry this out as a group for the challenge for Week 6.)

Learning From a Faithful Example (5 mins. / 10 mins.)

Read aloud the following portrait of Mother Teresa, a faithful example of love for the world.

Mother Teresa (Catholic nun)
(August 26, 1910 – September 5, 1997)

Mother Teresa said of herself, "By blood, I am Albanian. By citizenship, an Indian. By faith, I am a Catholic nun. As to my calling, I belong to the world. As to my heart, I belong entirely to the Heart of Jesus Christ."[7] Born in 1910 in Skopje, she was baptized Gonxha Agnes. With the world in her eye, at the age of eighteen, Gonxha left her home to become a missionary. She joined the Sisters of Loreto in Ireland and received the name Sister Mary Teresa after St. Thérèse of Lisieux. A few months later, she departed for Calcutta, India, where she taught at a school for girls for twenty years. In 1937, Sister Teresa made her Final Profession of Vows, and from that time on was called Mother Teresa.

On September 10, 1946, during a train ride, Mother Teresa received what she called her "call within a call." From that point on, as Jesus revealed to her the desire of his heart, she felt called as she never had before to serve the poorest of the poor. After two years of testing and discernment, Mother Teresa felt called to begin; on December 21, 1948, she entered the Calcutta slums for the first time. She washed the sores of children, visited families, and nursed a woman dying of tuberculosis. She began each day by taking Communion, and went out, rosary in hand, to serve Christ in the "least of these." After a few months, she was joined by a number of former students.

By the early 1960s, Mother Teresa began sending her sisters to other parts of India to help those in need. She later opened homes for the poor in Venezuela, Rome, Tanzania, and by the 1990s, in every continent. Mother Teresa was awarded the Nobel Peace Prize in 1979, honoring her work, as she called, "for the glory of God and in the name of the poor." At the time of her death in 1997, Mother Teresa's sisters numbered nearly 4,000 and were established in 610 foundations in 123 countries worldwide.[8]

Journaling Prayer
(10 mins. – *90-minute session only*)

Each person will need a notebook or journal and a pen. Have everyone spread out in the room and find a comfortable posture for writing. Play a worshipful song appropriate to the week's theme, setting the CD player or MP3 player on repeat; or play several songs to fill the time. Instruct participants to write in their notebooks or journals in response to the following two prayer prompts, allowing the Holy Spirit to lead their journaling. (Write the prayer prompts on a board or chart.)

Lord, you are giving me a "world in my eye" for . . .

This means that . . .

A Challenge (3 mins.)

Have participants turn to p. 186 in *A Faithful Heart* and review the challenge for Week 7.

Closing (2 mins.)

Close with a prayer or benediction, such as the following:

> *Peace be to the whole community, and love with faith, from God the Father and the Lord Jesus Christ. Grace be with all who have an undying love for our Lord Jesus Christ. (Ephesians 6:23-24)*

---

[7] Mother Teresa of Calcutta Center; http://www.motherteresa.org/.
[8] Mother Teresa of Calcutta Center.

Session

7

Learning:
Discipleship as a
Lifelong Adventure

Challenge for Week 7

This week, go on an inward adventure following Jesus. Examine your own faith more deeply through spiritual practices such as prayer, Bible study, and small-group discussion. While on "adventure," make note of what demands courage, what challenges you, what gives you joy.

Session 7
Learning: Discipleship as a Lifelong Adventure

Suggested times are noted in parentheses. The first time is for a 60-minute session; the second time is for a 90-minute session. (If only one time is given, that time applies to both formats.) Note that Journaling Prayer is added to the 90-minute session.

Opening (5 mins.)

Welcome participants and open with prayer. Use the prayer provided below, or offer an original prayer:

Lord Jesus, your call to your disciples is the same through all the ages: "Come, follow me." You don't tell us what lies ahead on the journey; you only promise that you will be with us every step of the way, and that it will be an exciting adventure with rewards greater than anything we could imagine. Give us courage for the journey. Help us to trust you with all our hearts, knowing beyond a shadow of a doubt that you are always leading the way and holding us with your right hand. Amen.

Invite participants to briefly share their experiences with the challenge for Week 7.

Looking Into God's Word (15 mins. / 20 mins.)

Read the following aloud:

To be a disciple of Jesus Christ requires following wherever he leads. Jesus said to his disciples,

> *If anyone wishes to come after Me, he must deny himself, and take up his cross and follow Me. (Matthew 16:24, NASB)*

According to this verse, discipleship involves self-denial, suffering, and uncertainty. It sounds risky and even dangerous. And it is! Being a follower of Jesus is an adventure, and every adventure has some element of risk. After all, that's what makes it an adventure.

Adventures, however, are also exciting, exhilarating, and extremely rewarding. Hear what Jesus had to say about taking up your cross and following him.

Have someone read aloud Matthew 10:38-39.

Losing your life doesn't sound very promising, does it? But we have to look past the literal meaning to find the real meaning. Hear these same verses from *The Message*:

> *If your first concern is to look after yourself, you'll never find yourself. But if you forget about yourself and look to me, you'll find both yourself and me. (Matthew 10:39)*

When we say *Yes* to the adventure of following Jesus, we are not losers but winners, finding more than we ever imagined.

In *The Message* we read,

> [*The Master*] *said, "That's what I mean: Risk your life and get more than you ever dreamed of. Play it safe and end up holding the bag." (Luke 19:26)*

Despite the rewards, it takes courage to step out into the un-known. The adventure of all adventures—following Jesus—is not for the faint-hearted. That is why God has given us so many words of encouragement.

Choose three people to read aloud the following verses:

Proverbs 3:5
Isaiah 41:13
Matthew 28:20

Briefly Discuss:
* What other verses from the Bible give you encour-agement and hope for the adventure of discipleship?

Have the women take turns reading verses aloud and shar-ing how these verses have given them courage and hope.

Discussing the Week's Reading
(15 mins. / 20 mins.)

This week's readings have focused on the lifelong adventure of learning what it means to be a disciple of Jesus Christ.

Choose from the following discussion questions:
1. Is there something you very much want to do that goes against tradition, popular opinion, or so-called "common sense"? What is it?

2. Would you describe Mary's journey with Jesus to be an adventure? Is your journey with Jesus an adventure? Have you ever connected with Mary's suffering in any way?

3. How has your faith adventure helped you to see the beauty of humanity and the world by following Jesus? How has it helped you to find the courage to face it?

4. What have you always wanted to do in following Jesus? What keeps you from doing it?

5. What would it take to be on that adventure with Jesus that helps you see the beauty, but also requires the courage of faith?

6. Have you ever gone on an inward adventure following Jesus, being pushed to examine your faith more deeply through prayer, Bible study, small-group discussion, or exploration of others' beliefs? What was it like? What took courage? How was your life disturbed? What gave you joy?

7. How is a marriage a daring adventure? How is being single a daring adventure? How is raising a child a daring adventure? How do these "common" but daring relationships teach us the beauty and draw from us the courage to live our lives as an adventure with each other and Jesus?

8. What does it mean to trust God with all your heart and not rely on your own understanding? When have you had to do this recently?

9. When you are uncertain of the path ahead, how do you trust to take the next steps?

Exploring Together (15 mins. / 20 mins.)

Have the women break into pairs, choosing a partner whose faith story she has never heard. Have them take turns telling about their adventure with Christ thus far on life's journey, as well as their dreams for what lies ahead. Write the following questions on a board or chart to help direct their sharing:

- When did you say *Yes* to following Jesus?
- In what ways has your faith journey been an adventure?
- What has been the greatest challenge or risk on your faith adventure so far?
- What has given you the courage and strength you have needed for the journey?
- What dreams and hopes for the future has God placed in your heart?

(60-minute groups will have approximately 7 minutes for each woman to share; 90-minute groups will have 10 minutes each.)

Learning From a Faithful Example (5 mins. / 10 mins.)

Read aloud the following portrait of Rosa Parks, a faithful example of a lifelong commitment to the adventure of discipleship.

Rosa Parks (civil rights activist)
(February 4, 1913 – October 24, 2005)

December 1, 1955, marks what many historians date as the beginning of the modern civil rights movement in the

United States. This was the day when an unknown seamstress in Montgomery, Alabama, refused to give up her seat on a bus to a white passenger. This woman was Rosa Parks. She was arrested and fined for violating a city ordinance, but the incident led to the formation of the Montgomery Improvement Association, led by Dr. Martin Luther King, Jr. The association called for a boycott of the city-owned bus company, which lasted 382 days and brought Mrs. Parks, Dr. King, and their cause to the world's attention. A Supreme Court Decision struck down the Montgomery ordinance under which Mrs. Parks had been fined, and outlawed racial segregation on public transportation.

In 1957, Mrs. Parks and her husband moved to Detroit, Michigan. In 1964, she became a deaconess in the African Methodist Episcopal Church. After the death of her husband in 1977, Mrs. Parks founded the Rosa and Raymond Parks Institute for Self-Development. The Institute sponsors an annual summer program for teenagers called "Pathways to Freedom." Through the program, young people tour the country in buses, tracing the path of the Underground Railroad, learning the history of the United States and of the civil rights movement. Among her honors, Rosa Parks was voted by *Time Magazine* as one of the 100 most influential people of the twentieth century, and she received both the Presidential Medal of Freedom in 1996 and a Congressional Gold Medal in 1999.

Journaling Prayer
(10 mins. – *90-minute session only*)

Each person will need a notebook or journal and a pen. Have everyone spread out in the room and find a comfortable posture for writing. Play a worshipful song appropriate to the week's theme, setting the CD player or MP3 player on repeat; or play several songs to fill the time. Instruct participants to write in their notebooks or journals in response to the following three prayer prompts, allowing the Holy Spirit to lead their journaling. (Write the prayer prompts on a board or chart.)

Lord, when I think about the adventure of following you wherever you lead, I am excited about . . .

I admit that I am uncertain about . . .

What gives me courage for the journey ahead is . . .

A Challenge (3 mins.)

Have participants turn to p. 212 in *A Faithful Heart* and review the challenge for Week 8.

Closing (2 mins.)

Close with a prayer or benediction, such as the following:

> *Those who trust in the LORD are like Mount Zion,*
> *which cannot be moved, but abides forever.*
> *As the mountains surround Jerusalem,*
> *so the LORD surrounds his people,*
> *from this time on and forevermore. (Psalm 125:1-2)*

Session

8

Authentic:
Living in Loving,
Healthy Relationships

Challenge for Week 8

This week, practice forgiveness.
Think of a hurt you are holding
onto, and imagine you are looking at
the person(s) who hurt you through
"forgiveness glasses"—with new
eyes. Write your own prayer for the
person(s) who wronged you.

Session 8
Authentic: Living in Loving, Healthy Relationships

Suggested times are noted in parentheses. The first time is for a 60-minute session; the second time is for a 90-minute session. (If only one time is given, that time applies to both formats.) Note that Journaling Prayer is added to the 90-minute session.

Opening (5 mins.)

Welcome participants and open with prayer. Use the prayer provided below, or offer an original prayer:

Loving God, we long to have loving, healthy relationships, and we know this is what you desire for us. The key is to love others as we love ourselves, just as Jesus taught us. But sometimes this is not easy. Relationships can be so complicated—and painful. Help us to forgive those who have hurt us, extending the same mercy and grace that you have extended to us. Teach us to love even our enemies, Lord. Give us the ability to love and accept all people just as you do. What seems impossible to us is possible with you. Amen.

Invite participants to briefly share their experiences with the challenge for Week 8.

Looking Into God's Word (15 mins. / 20 mins.)

Read the following aloud:

When Jesus was asked what is the greatest commandment, this was his response:

> *Jesus answered, "The first is, '. . . you shall love the Lord your God with all your heart, and with all your soul, and with all your mind, and with all your strength.' The second is this, 'You shall love your neighbor as yourself.' There is no other commandment greater than these."*
> *(Mark 12:29-31)*

Loving God and loving our neighbor go hand in hand. Loving God means loving our neighbor as well. In fact, the apostle John said that if we do not love others, we are not loving God.

Have someone read aloud 1 John 4:20.

Often it seems so much more difficult to love our neighbors than it does to love God, doesn't it? How can we have healthy, loving relationships with others when they can be so difficult to get along with sometimes? The Bible gives us some practical guidelines. In the Book of James, we read this:

> *Make this your common practice: Confess your sins to each other and pray for each other so that you can live together whole and healed. (James 5:16, The Message)*

Likewise, the apostle Paul gives us this instruction:

> *Be kind to one another, tenderhearted, forgiving one an-*
> *other, as God in Christ has forgiven you. (Ephesians 4:32)*

God knows that relationships can be difficult and complicated. That is why God tells us that we are to make confession, forgiveness, and prayer regular parts of relating to one
another. These practices help us to build and maintain
whole, healthy relationships.

Briefly Discuss:
- Why do you think confession, forgiveness, and
  prayer are critical to healthy relationships?
- Do you pray regularly for those who are part of your
  life—including the difficult people? Why or why
  not?

We may be willing to follow these instructions for those we
love, but what about those we struggle to love? Jesus said
we are to treat others as we want to be treated.

Have someone read aloud Matthew 7:12.

But Jesus didn't stop there. He said we are to love even our
enemies.

Read aloud Matthew 5:44-48 from *The Message*:

> *I'm telling you to love your enemies. Let them bring out*
> *the best in you, not the worst. When someone gives you a*
> *hard time, respond with the energies of prayer, for then you*
> *are working out of your true selves, your God-created*

selves. This is what God does. . . . If all you do is love the
lovable, do you expect a bonus? Anybody can do that. If
you simply say hello to those who greet you, do you expect
a medal? Any run-of-the-mill sinner does that. In a word,
what I'm saying is, Grow up. You're kingdom subjects.
Now live like it. Live out your God-created identity. Live
generously and graciously toward others, the way God
lives toward you. (Matthew 5:44-48)

Briefly Discuss:
- What "struck" you in these verses? What stood out?

Remembering how gracious and merciful God is toward us is what enables us to extend grace and mercy to others—whether they be loved ones or enemies. When we find it difficult to love or forgive others, let us meditate on the amazing love and unmerited forgiveness we receive so freely and abundantly from God.

Discussing the Week's Reading (15 mins. / 20 mins.)

This week's readings have focused on how to engage in loving, healthy relationships with a variety of people throughout the dynamic experiences of life.

Choose from the following discussion questions:
1. Think about the complicated relationships in your life. How do they match the complications that Mary had in her relationships? What could you learn from Mary?
2. What have you learned from your faith community in terms of healthy relationships?
3. When someone hurts you, do you expect that you will get to a place of forgiveness toward that person?

With or without that person's help? With or without the help of a community of faith?

4. When was a time that it was difficult for you to forgive? Where did you get the strength to do it?

5. How would things be different in your church—and in your community—if your church were known to be a community of forgiveness and reconciliation?

6. Why is forgiveness central to what it means to be a follower of Jesus? Has forgiveness been a central part of *your* faith commitment? Why or why not?

7. How were you taught to forgive—or not to forgive?

8. What do you think a healthy apology is? When have you experienced one?

9. Why is it often difficult to love and accept others as they are? What can help us to do this?

10. Think of a difficult relationship in your life right now. How could praying for this person and asking God to help you see him/her through God's eyes change the situation?

11. How can following the Golden Rule help us to love others as Jesus commanded?

12. What were the three simple rules of John Wesley, and how can they help us to have loving, healthy relationships?

Exploring Together (15 mins. / 20 mins.)

Read aloud these verses from *The Message*:

Welcome with open arms fellow believers who don't see things the way you do. And don't jump all over them every time they do or say something you don't agree with—even when it seems that they are strong on opinions but weak in the faith department. Remember, they have their own history

to deal with. Treat them gently. . . . So where does that leave
you when you criticize a brother? And where does that leave
you when you condescend to a sister? I'd say it leaves you
looking pretty silly—or worse. Eventually, we're all going
to end up kneeling side by side in the place of judgment, fac-
ing God. Your critical and condescending ways aren't going
to improve your position there one bit. (Romans 14:1, 10-11)

The "motto" of The United Methodist Church is "Open Hearts, Open Minds, Opens Doors." What do you think this means?

Allow for brief discussion.

How do the verses we read from Romans help to inform our understanding of what it means to have open hearts, open minds, and open doors?

Allow for brief discussion.

Brainstorm a list of habits or characteristics of a welcoming, accepting church, listing them on a board or chart.

What insights can we gain from this list for helping us to have healthy, loving relationships in our personal lives?

Allow for brief discussion.

Learning From a Faithful Example
(5 mins. / 10 mins.)

Read aloud the following portrait of Corrie ten Boom, a faithful example of authenticity and love—even love for her enemies.

Corrie ten Boom (Dutch Christian Holocaust survivor)
(April 15, 1892 – April 15, 1983)

Corrie ten Boom was born in Holland in 1892. She was the youngest of three sisters and one brother. Their father, Casper, was a watchmaker, and he raised his family to be very devoted Christians. During the Second World War, the ten Boom family home became a hiding place for fugitives of the Nazis—Jews and the Dutch Underground. Corrie became a ringleader within the Underground network, finding other courageous Dutch families who would also help and house refugees. This non-violent resistance against the Nazis was the ten Booms' way of living out their Christian faith. However, on February 28, 1944, the family was betrayed, and Gestapo raided the ten Boom home arresting Corrie; her father; her sisters, Betsie and Nollie; her brother, Willem; and her nephew, Peter. Fortunately, the refugees hiding in the false wall in Corrie's bedroom remained safely hidden from the Gestapo and were successfully rescued forty-seven hours later by Resistance workers.

Corrie spent ten months in three different prisons, the last being the infamous Ravensbruck Concentration Camp near Berlin, Germany. She would be the only member of her family to survive the war. At age fifty-three, Corrie began a worldwide ministry spanning sixty countries over the next thirty-three years of her life, testifying about what she and her sister Betsie had learned at Ravensbruck: "There is no pit so deep that God's love is not deeper still!" and "God will give us the love to be able to forgive our enemies."[9] Corrie ten Boom died on her ninety-first birthday.

Journaling Prayer
(10 mins. – *90-minute session only*)

Each person will need a notebook or journal and a pen. Have everyone spread out in the room and find a comfortable posture for writing. Play a worshipful song appropriate to the week's theme, setting the CD player or MP3 player on repeat; or play several songs to fill the time. Instruct participants to write in their notebooks or journals in response to the following three prayer prompts, allowing the Holy Spirit to lead their journaling. (Write the prayer prompts on a board or chart.)

Lord, when I search my heart, I realize I am still harboring resentment and bitterness toward . . .

To forgive this person/these persons, I need to . . .

To have healthy, loving relationships in my life, I sense you calling me to . . .

A Challenge (3 mins.)

To close the study, give the participants this final challenge:

This study is coming to a close, but your journey to have a faithful heart continues. Let this final challenge be your continual practice. At the end of each day, review your actions and attitudes in light of the three simple rules[10] of Wesleyan living:

Do no harm, do good, and stay in love with God.

Closing (2 mins.)

Close with a prayer or benediction, such as the following:

[May] your love . . . overflow more and more with knowledge and full insight to help you to determine what is best, so that in the day of Christ you may be pure and blameless, having produced the harvest of righteousness that comes through Jesus Christ for the glory and praise of God.
(Philippians 1:9-11)

[9] Corrie ten Boom Museum "The Hiding Place"; http://www.corrietenboom.com/history.htm.
[10] Rueben P. Job, *Three Simple Rules: A Wesleyan Way of Living* (Abingdon Press, 2007).

Coming in December 2010

from Abingdon Press

A Hopeful Earth
by Sally Dyck and Sarah Ehrman

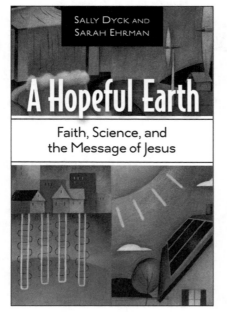

In this unique study, a bishop and a young science teacher ask the questions, "Who are we?" and "Why are we interested in connecting Jesus to the care of creation?"

ISBN: 9781426710377
$ 10.00

 **Abingdon Press**

Also Available:

A Hopeful Earth Leader Guide
9781426710414
$7.00

**A Hopeful Earth
Downloadable Leader Guide**
9781426713934
$5.00